BUDGETING
DOESN'T HAVE TO
SUCK

For Young Adults Who
Want More Money

JIM MILLER

Budgeting Doesn't Have to Suck:
For Young Adults Who Want More Money
2ⁿᵈ Edition

Copyright © 2013, 2020 RMWP
https://iamjimmiller.com

ISBN: 978-0-9891967-0-3
Library of Congress Control Number: 2013903472

Disclaimers:
Nothing in this book constitutes investment advice.

Published By:
RMW PUBLISHING
https://rmwp.org

PRINTED IN THE UNITED STATES OF AMERICA

First Revised Edition

DEDICATED TO MY DAD,
IN ABSENTIA,
ON HIS 75TH BIRTHDAY,
17 APRIL 2013.

TABLE OF CONTENTS

PREFACE

Welcome to the first second edition of this book. (That made sense, right?) By no means is the first edition of this book invalid. There is no advice in the original edition that I wouldn't still give. So why?

I fixed a few typos and style issues. I updated the subtitle. And I added a lot of new content. The main reason, though, is that the world has changed a lot since I released *Budgeting Doesn't Have to Suck* in 2013, and I want to provide you with those updates in this expanded version.

As I write this preface, the year is 2020 and it is summer. We're in month three of the coronavirus pandemic and trying to understand how it will impact our future. Much is unknown and much more is speculated.

The economy is bouncing back quite well right now, thanks to government stimulus programs. Without a vaccine or treatment, as well as a shift backwards in the types of goods and services consumers are spending their money on, we may be in a challenging spot for years to come.

Wherever the world moves, and however you move in the world, it has never been more important to understand what you value in life and how to best aim your money plan toward those values.

I want you to be as prepared as you can be. That is why I wrote and released this second expanded edition. I hope you enjoy it, and that this book helps the future you to be even more awesome.

Only the Best,

Jim Miller
Los Angeles, CA
June 2020

INTRODUCTION

WHY ANOTHER PERSONAL FINANCE BOOK?

The world is filled with books on personal finance, budgeting, and well-known ways to protect and grow our hard-earned money. Why write yet another one? First of all, my exploration of personal finance and budgeting skips past much of the knowledge that the general public already knows. And with so many voices out there, I want to give people the right information as clearly as possible.

This book is not "for dummies," and instead gets to the point, so you can learn everything you need to know without me wasting your valuable time. You already know it's financially smarter to buy a used car than a new car. You already know that you shouldn't eat out as often as you'd like to. You already know that you should save more money than you might already be saving.

But what do you know about getting more money? What do you know about growing yourself? What do you know about automating your financial life so you have greater success and spend less time dealing with it?

You may be picking up this book in uncertain times. Maybe you have debt or you lost your job or had a big unexpected expense and have nothing. Or, maybe you're crushing it right now and are seeking new strategies so you can grow even faster. To all of you, you are holding the right book in your hand.

In this book, there are no end-of-chapter checklists, no worksheets, and no quizzes. There is only tremendously helpful advice that will help motivated people like you gain control, get more money, and have a better life. Does that mean you have to love budgeting? No. Keep reading.

I have been working in finance, accounting and with numbers for over twenty years, and I am going to share all of my best advice with you in this concise manuscript. And it's not all about spending less. That would suck!

Consistently for many years, I have avoided bad debt, diversified and increased my income, increased savings and my investments, given to non-profit and social causes and every strategy that I use is in this book.

I am not cheap at all. I spend money on things that matter to me. But I am definitely frugal, or careful, as to where my money goes. For example, buying high-quality food is important to me. Clothing, not so much. I have a quality, but small wardrobe. I don't want too many decisions.

Instead of taking my car to a car wash, I wash it myself for $4 at one of those high-pressure, do-it-yourself places. I then air-dry my car on the drive home, along the coast of Los Angeles, at a safe but irresponsible speed. You get the picture. I save so I have more money to invest.

A primary concept in this book is that managing and growing your money can be fun. The aim of this book is to give you the right tools now so that when you are crushing it you keep it. I will show you that this can be fun.

Making your money process easy is crucial—else it will not be fun, and you will not do it. I'm talking about real fun. Living life, planning and making space for the things you value the most.

I will provide the philosophical and technical tools for you to create your own ways to gain control of your finances and to start a way of thinking that leads to financial success.

This book is that inspirational, one-hour meeting that starts on time and ends with you feeling supercharged and ready to act.

My readers are those who desire to circumvent relearning what they already know and to discover something unique; to efficiently gain insight that can make their lives better.

This kind of knowledge is esoteric and practical. Those wanting to know these topics in complete detail are invited to peruse the 200+ page workbooks they can find at every bookstore.

This is not to say that there is no detail in my writing. Such detail has been my routine for over two decades. But the detail lies hidden here, primarily, while what is writ large is the philosophy and strategy on how to have a better future.

I am grateful to my father, Dr. Ron Miller, for wordlessly teaching me about the book writing and publishing world, a world I entered after his death in order to continue his many works and publications.

I also want to thank my son, Jetson, for allowing me the time to write this book. Today is his first birthday (2013). He teaches me every single day.

BUDGETING DOESN'T HAVE TO SUCK

STARTING ON EMPTY

WHEN YOU HAVE NADA

This chapter is new to the second expanded edition. When the first edition of this book was released it was 2013 and the economy was doing okay. Unemployment was low. At the time of this writing, it is the summer of 2020 and the government is not allowing many businesses to function. Millions of good people are without jobs. A lot of people need help.

Coronavirus or not, if you are in a murky place financially, this chapter is for you. If you are willing to get busy and to take responsibility for your life, there is absolutely a brighter path ahead for you. Read this book entirely.

This chapter is unique and will appear like a list or guide, because it is. Many of the items within will be explored further in later chapters. But I want to help those in need immediately before we journey any further.

IF YOU JUST LOST YOUR JOB

File for unemployment benefits if that is an option. Get this done right away since many states have significant delays. Be aware though that you will owe income taxes on the money you receive. And if severance is an option, have that hard conversation and politely ask for it.

Fight to maintain your insurance. Health, vehicle, renters, owners, earthquake… do your best to keep your coverage current. If you can't afford COBRA or medical insurance, apply for Medicaid. Most states have programs that can help you. If you can adjust your insurance coverage down, that can save money while still keeping you covered. Find a way to keep your insurance.

Get rid of everything you don't need and do it right now. How many TV subscriptions are you paying for? Can your restaurant spend be replaced with homemade meals? How much do you like that friend living on your sofa?

Maybe hit pause on things like your gym membership until you're back on track and workout from home instead. Make changes to stop the bleeding today to give yourself more flexibility down the road. Go through your last few bank and credit card statements to see where the money went. Evaluate everything.

Sell anything you can. Do you need two cars? Maybe that "thing" you bought at 1:30am two months ago would be better off in someone else's home. Get creative and clean house.

Build or maintain your emergency fund. Even if you're on unemployment, get your expenses to a level where you have at least one month of living expenses in a savings account. This is as psychological as it is financial. Once you have a little cushion, cut the emergency savings contributions until you have the discretionary income (i.e. – the spare cash) to continue.

If you're fortunate enough to have a 401k or similar retirement account, it often seems attractive to borrow from it. Try to avoid this as any accumulation of debt and/or reduction in retirement savings is bad. Borrow from your 401k as a last resort, but before touching your emergency fund if more than a few hundred dollars.

Avoid bad credit by proactively reaching out to your creditors, utilities, landlord or mortgage company. By notifying these entities of your change in income, they may offer opportunities that can help you. If you miss a payment, you can also ask that it not be reported to the credit bureaus. This will likely only work if you had a flawless payment record prior to your job loss. These programs will buy you valuable time and allow you to preserve your credit even during bad times. Stay ahead of these problems so they don't become bigger problems. Don't be ashamed to ask. People like to help people.

Consider moving in with friends/family. Or take on a

roommate. Or move to a city or state with a lower cost of living. There are many stories of people here in Los Angeles moving to Texas, Arizona, Oregon and Utah. Not everyone lost their job, some people just retired to these places or wanted to live in a place with a lower cost of living. The point is that if you lost your job or source of income, every aspect of your life should be on the table and that includes your location.

START CLIMBING THE STAIRS

Notice I did not tell you to start climbing the ladder. Because this is not about climbing someone else's ladder. This is about you finding *you* and being happy and getting more money. You will be building the staircase from the ground and then climbing your own staircase to the top.

Having a strong network is maybe the most important element to your future success. Think of a genuine and diverse network as you would an emergency cash fund.

Help people as often as you can and when you need a favor, there will be people waiting to help. This doesn't mean you have to be an extrovert either. You can network completely online.

What if you just lost your job and have no network? Then it's time to get started. Use LinkedIn or other tools to find connections in the industry or company that you want to be a part of. Research to find something you and this person have in common. If not a common friend, maybe it is an experience you shared (i.e. – sharing a previous boss) or a career change. Find something similar and include that in your communication when you reach out. Remember, the best way to build connections is to ask people about themselves and their experience.

Set short and long-term goals. Use the notes app on your phone. Your goal list should be the first and last thing you look at each day. Have a section for "tomorrow" goals, "this week" goals, "this year" goals and "next year" goals.

Tracking goals in this way can change your life quickly!

Eat quality food. I get it. You just lost your job and you're calling me bad names in your head. But healthy food will make you more productive than junk food. Buy a whole chicken and it will last you a few days. Make some wraps with leftovers! Replace soda with water. Eating clean absolutely does not need to cost more than junk food.

Create instead of consume! Turn off the streams and make a video of your new vision and who you're working hard to become. Share the video with friends. Draw, paint, take photos, write music using a free app, create an exercise plan and share it, start a blog… all free (or mostly free) things to move your mind from consumer to creator.

Exercise, wake up early, make new habits. This is all part of the process that will change your luck and connect you to a better future. This one costs zero dollars. In return, you will be more focused, more energetic, have less or no anxiety and have stronger will power. Move to get your energy, strength and creativity strong.

Read a lot of books. You're already here and on your way. If every book or podcast you listen to gives you even one great idea or teaches you one powerful lesson, just think of who you can be in one year with a good reading habit.

Generate multiple streams of income. Get out of the situation where 100% of your income is based on trading your time for money. You want to earn income while you sleep. Work towards getting a new job and simultaneously improve your skills in the job that you have or want.

If you're a food server, find videos, seminars or master classes on customer service and management so you can grow your career. If you're a marketer, read a Seth Godin book and watch the thousands of free marketing videos out there. So much self-learning available.

Start another stream of income or side hustle. I'm personally not a big fan of the worn-out term "side hustle" but it means having something you do outside of your employment that earns income. Usually something you find enjoyable. And, if you work hard enough, your side hustle can become your primary source of income as it has for many others just like you.

Here are 10 side hustle examples to get your mind going:

- Make items and sell them on Etsy
- Walk pets or house sit
- Buy, fixup and sell things (furniture)
- Monetize social media (YouTube, Instagram)
- Virtual event planning for businesses
- Rent out extra space (parking spots, a room)
- Freelance your job skills after-hours
- Teach online (English, music)
- Convert VHS tapes into digital formats
- Write a book! (even an e-book)

There is a lot to do and you can enjoy the journey. You have a choice today, regardless of how good or bad you have it... you can eat junk food, drink too much, consume endlessly and believe that it's okay to be idle and feel sorry for yourself.

Or you can get pumped, work on being a stronger person and be the next success story. Being the best version of you will attract better relationships and completely change your luck. If you apply yourself and do what is in this book, this will work for you. Believe in yourself!

LAY IT ALL OUT

WHY ARE YOU DOING THIS?

I promise that this book will be as concise as can be, but you need to learn to drive a stick shift before you can speed off in a sports car. You need to learn to walk in heels before you jump on the dance floor. And even if you already know how to drive a stick shift (like I do), and how to walk in heels (like I do; okay, not really), the road you're going to travel will be a new one.

Whatever your situation may be, the first thing to acknowledge is that there is only one person responsible for your financial reality and that is you! Do not blame anyone else or anything else. And do not give credit for your overall success to anyone else, either. That includes a big bull market where everyone is suddenly an "expert" investor.

You are the controller of the many variables that got you here, and wherever you are, this book will lead you to opportunities and reveal ideas that will allow you to create your ideal financial future. The more attention you give something, the more likely you will succeed.

There is nothing wrong with wherever you are financially, and it is never too late to completely change where you are heading. I have seen countless people of all ages turn their financial futures around completely. That you're reading this book shows that you are ready to get to work, and that puts you ahead of so many. Let's keep going.

MONEY & SELF-CONTROL

There is a close link between spending habits and self-control. Do you spend money now or save for tomorrow, and how do you make these decisions? You already know that self-control has its good days and its bad days, too.

The best way to start making better decisions with money is to have a budget; there is nothing more critical. As with a workout schedule, you need a plan. A budget forces you to have a plan to accommodate all of your needs, some of your wants, and a pathway into the future.

There are several ways to define self-control, but the central tenet of the concept is the ability to overcome short-term temptations in order to achieve long-term goals. There are many good resources on self-control and building better habits, and I strongly recommend you look them up. My personal favorite author on this topic is James Clear. His book "Atomic Habits" is genius.

Some of us are better at this than others, and you need to first have a long-term goal or a plan. Then, managing and growing your money will become a habit. Without this long-term plan, having good habits simply means avoiding all fun. And that is the opposite of reality, and of what I have to suggest.

As you sculpt your long-term plan, you'll know more

clearly that, "Hey, if I buy these Coachella tickets, I'll need to spend less on clothes for the next two months so that I stay within budget and achieve my goal of having a down payment for a house in two years."

Without this long-term plan, the realization could go more like this: "Cool, I have $800 in credit available on my credit card. I'm in, and let's rent a vacation house with a pool too, because Tent City blows!"

The goal in budgeting is to have a plan. Not a perfect plan, but a plan. And in that plan you can make room for the things you love. That includes lattes and Coachella tickets, and anything else that is important to your true self. Once you set freedoms in your budget, you will never feel guilty about spending.

OKAY, GET YOURSELF A DRINK

Happiness comes by doing difficult things, and step one

of anything is always the most difficult, yet also the most important. There's no way around it.

This process is a required first step if you're in good financial shape, too, but by the end of this exercise you will know everything. as they say, knowing is half the battle.

This stands in the world of personal finance, too. I prefer a little wine for this brainstorm. Maybe you prefer tea, or tequila shots…whatever gets you through it. I promise this will be the fastest exercise in this book.

The first step of course is to identify all key issues and goings-on with your finances, the ins and outs of your cash. You're not mapping out a budget, here. You're making some honest notes. You can do this on a piece of paper, on your computer, or on your phone. It doesn't matter.

What matters is that you do it and are honest with yourself. This is a mental exercise, above all else, and by the end of it, you will feel accomplished.

Almost every book on business contains a sentence with a similar meaning to this: "If you think it and authentically believe it, you will achieve it." And in order to achieve our ideal financial condition, and to sculpt our ideal financial future, like a puzzle, you need to lay it all out before you can put it together.

IF YA GOT IT, GOOD

If your finances are in order and you are not carrying a burdening debt load, then congratulations, because this step will be a little less stressful for you. There will be just as much to think about, however.

The process involves realigning your expenses with your values, reducing expenses, maximizing income, finding new income opportunities that earn money while you sleep, automating your savings and investments, growing as an individual, and planning for the future. You stand to gain as much from this book as anyone else.

Most importantly, although you may have kept your finances in rock star shape, there is a child, a parent, a friend, a classmate, a coworker…someone who needs your help. This book will give you tools, strategies, and concepts to share. And what classier gift to give than a book?

IF YA GOT IT BAD

Good news! You have learned the most fundamental lesson, and it is that not having control of your finances sucks. You have been burned and you're about to learn how to avoid this from happening again in the future.

Are your car payments behind? Do you feel nauseous

thinking about that credit card balance? Do you have a collector calling you from some parking tickets you decided to ignore in 1996? I promise you that it will get better if you want it to. I've helped people do it, and I can help you, too.

A guy recently came to me and confessed that he had failed to file his taxes for the last four years. He was being paid pretax dollars as an independent contractor, and the money was gone before tax season arrived.

Like so many people, their personal finances become a source of depression, and human nature puts a wall between us and the situation. The difficulty with this, of course, is that the problem becomes increasingly worse as it nears our fiscal cliff.

The advice I gave this person is the same advice everyone would give anyone when they were avoiding an issue that had a negative effect on their life, and that is to immediately admit and address the problem at hand.

I wish I had this book at the time, because I would have told him, "Read my book!" Instead I advised him to lay it all out and call me when he was ready to make changes.

I also gave him the name of a company that helps people who are behind on their taxes and negotiates with the governmental agencies on their behalf. He is now on a path to getting on track and putting the mess behind him forever.

The absolutely most notable thing to remember, here, is that financial disaster happens to good people. Financial disaster happens to smart people. In many ways, the financial system is designed for you to lose, and there are plenty of opportunities to commit blunders. This is precisely why I'm writing this book. I'm writing it to share what I've learned and what I've seen work, so that what has happened to others doesn't happen to you.

Remember that if you're ashamed of your finances today, that's okay. You're not an idiot. You're not a terrible person. People all around you have been where you are now. You are reading this book to make a change, and you are about to have the tools necessary to accomplish your goals.

MAKE CHANGES

STARTING TODAY

Whether you're the person living paycheck to paycheck or the person looking for new financial strategies, there are changes you can make today that will benefit you in the future.

This is where most books will tell you to cut out everything that you enjoy in life, to knit your own clothing, and to watch your pennies. While you're at it, replace high-quality food with porridge and suddenly three ghosts are visiting you in the middle of the night telling you how much you suck.

The reason that advice is terrible is that everyone is different. Everyone's financial situation is different, and what everyone values is different.

A single person might prefer restaurants and new clothes more than a parent would. A parent might prefer having money for their children's schooling and tickets to Disneyland over a large closet full of the fanciest handbags.

There are too many variables, and so this chapter, more than the others, will give you the tools for you to decide what is most valued in your life.

The first question you should ask yourself is, what are you spending money on that you don't need? Second, what are you spending money on that is unhealthy? And third, what are you spending money on that contradicts your values and goals?

THINGS YOU DON'T NEED

Things you don't need should be easy to identify, and are the things I mentioned in the introduction that most of us already know. Review everything, starting with the big ticket items, such as mortgage, rent and car payments.

Do you need two cars or could your household do just fine with one? Is refinancing or moving an option? Are there monthly expenses you can part with forever or for a period of time?

In the early days of my household, my wife and I knew we should be doing more productive things with our lives than watching TV. Even the basic cable TV package that we had was expensive. So, we called our cable provider and after a short, four-hour phone call, we finally got our cable TV cancelled.

We kept our Internet service and spent $100 on an Apple TV. We were then paying just $16 per month for digital apps. The Apple TV paid for itself in less than three months, and we were saving $40/mo from what we were paying with cable.

THINGS THAT ARE UNHEALTHY

I intentionally separate "things you don't need" from "things that are unhealthy," because for many people these are not mutually exclusive. It's crazy in the first place that so many people spend so much money on things that are not good for them.

The obvious ones are eating unhealthy meals at restaurants, and things like smoking or visiting too many happy hours. Additionally, anything you can't "not" do for seven consecutive days is probably unhealthy, and I'll tell you right now that you're wasting your money on it.

I'm not talking about removing anything from your life right now. But as a starting point, let's identify the unhealthy items and start thinking about what could be reduced or even axed in order to achieve our financial goals.

So you celebrate weekends like a Mormon and brown bag your work lunches. Does your diet have a lot of processed meat that could be swapped for beans? I would make a bad vegan (or its less gregarious cousin, vegetarian), but I consume very little processed meat these days, and even the red meat I eat is grass-fed and consumed in moderation. Changes like this can save you money while making you healthier.

One of my favorite food genres is Mexican fare, and I eat it as often as possible. You know when you're with your significant other and trying to figure out where to go for dinner and he replies, "Well, I had Mexican yesterday, so no Mexican." I never say that, even if I just ate it. And if I'm grabbing a quick lunch, then a vegetarian burrito saves me money, tastes just as wondrous, and benefits my health.

Do you pay for a gym membership, yet never seem to have time to go? Consider making yourself go three times per week. Or cancel the membership and work out at home instead. Perhaps this will give you less time to spend money doing other things such as shopping, eating out, or putting a few too many back after work.

THINGS THAT DON'T HELP YOU GROW

Getting control of your finances is an evaluation of your existence. What you value, where your money goes, and the choices you make today will connect you to your future.

You can tell a lot about a person, a company, a country, who they truly are, by looking at their budget. If a country spends more on their military than on education, this tells us something. If a person spends more on a car than on their rent or mortgage, this tells us something.

I'm not inferring anything here other than what one's expenditures can tell us. And this is essential to keep in mind as you create your budget, as you are also evidencing your values.

In this same vein, you can tell a lot about yourself by how you budget your time. Maybe you work, maybe you sleep, but it's what you do with your free time that counts. Think of your time working and sleeping as your inescapable fixed expenses, like rent and car payments. Think of your free time as your variable expenses, like restaurants and shopping. Both fixed and variable expenses have room for adjustment, but it's the variable expenses that allow the most movement.

You have total control over what you do with your free time. Do you spend it hanging out with friends? With your family and loved ones? Do you offer your time to a philanthropic organization, or help others who need it?

Are you more of a creator or a consumer? Are you the type of person who enjoys watching TV or the person who creates YouTube videos? Are you the type of person who buys all of your music, or the type who stays in one night per week and creates it?

It's much easier to be a consumer than it is to be a creator. The position here is not constant, though, and with self-control, positive habits, and conscious effort, you can move from one side of the spectrum to the other. Be a creator!

So what does this all have to do with budgeting, and why does this matter? It matters because at this stage you are defining yourself.

I am using the written word to drift your mind into realizing what matters to you the most. And once you establish that, you will be ready to create your budget and bring every facet of your life into line with your value system. You will be happier and more successful because of it. You will be on the more successful path.

We haven't delved into your actual budget, but off the top of your head, you should know if you're spending more on one category than another. And it's okay if you don't. Bringing your budget into alignment with your values can be a life-changing and transformative process.

IDENTIFY YOUR VALUES

WHAT DO YOU VALUE?

Some people think of budgeting as something that people without much money have to do. This is totally and completely wrong. The expression, "I'm on a budget," to imply a moment in time when someone is broke, has led to a lot of misinterpretation. Budgeting is for people who want to achieve their financial goals, whether they're wealthy or struggling.

I can tell you my net worth at any moment. People with the most money are notoriously the most prolific budgeters, even if that means they pay someone else to manage it for them.

Budgeting is an intensely personal and spiritual process, and to do it properly you need to explore who you are and what you are at your absolute core.

Do you know that person who drives a Mercedes, but

rents a shabby apartment and has massive credit card debt? I told myself in my twenties, "You can buy a high-end car once you own a house, maxed out your 401k match or retirement savings, maxed out your child(ren)'s college savings account, are absent of debt, support a cause, and have six months of emergency expenses saved."

Even today, I drive a really nice car that I am really grateful for, but it cost me less than a lot of people spend on their cars. (And don't lease your cars, either, unless it's through a business!) The point of this is that my budget and my spending show that I value family, long-term security, and freedom over what I drive.

In fact, in 2013, when I wrote the first edition of this book, I commuted around West LA on a 125cc scooter to save money and time. My wife drove our one car. I really miss that scooter, and am thankful that the vehicles of Los Angeles never ate me alive. It was a lot of fun to ride around, and I could park anywhere. That was a luxury to me. It saved me time. It gave me more time for life.

The fact is that the future is never guaranteed, and you need to first create and live by a budget that suits your finances today. Then, grow from there. And we will talk about that soon.

Your budget should only reflect your base income. Maybe you're expecting a hefty raise or a gigantic bonus, but don't include it.

The exception would be if a large piece of your income is from bonuses or commission—then include it in your income, but be conservative. Someday, when your income does increase, and you find yourself with more money available for your expenditures, investments, and savings, *good news*, because you get to choose the best way to spend it.

You need to avoid situations where the realization of future income goes immediately to paying off a previous overextension of your finances. Plan conservatively, and feel free to beat your budget as often as you can.

LOCATION, LOCATION, LOCATION

Budgets vary from person to person, and also from location to location. People in cold climates literally have a tax on winter that folks in Southern California get to avoid.

I grew up in suburban Chicago, where monthly heating costs are often hundreds of dollars. Houses and cars also age more rapidly there, due to the cold and salt.

Here in LA, our heaters might be turned on a handful of nights per year. If you live close to the ocean, you don't even need an air conditioner. So those savings help to offset the higher cost of living.

It's a study too ambitious for this book, but a fascinating discussion worthy of examination: what role does climate play on a household's economy in the short and long term?

Every location has its own cost of living. The cost of living is the amount of money you need to maintain your standard of living in a given location. Rent/mortgage, food, transportation, clothing, entertainment, equipment, education, and taxes are just some of the basic expenses that can fluctuate from place to place.

Big cities like Los Angeles or New York have high costs of living, due to exceptionally high state income taxes, along with high cost of rent and everything listed earlier. It's supply and demand.

Along with a higher cost of living, you should also be paid a higher wage. But this is not always the case.

You often hear about people leaving in flocks from high-cost-of-living places and taking their families to lower-cost-of-living places. A popular place for Californians to relocate to is Texas. Texas has no state income taxes, as of the time of this manuscript, and that seems like an immediate 13%+ savings on income versus California. But places like Texas make up for the lack of income taxes in other areas, such as sales taxes and property taxes. Be sure to look at the full picture before you move to your new paradise.

And before you hit send on that hate mail, yes, Texas does have a lower cost of living than places like Los Angeles, San Francisco, New York, Maui, and other crowded cities. Create an income stream before you make the move, though, if you're looking to have more discretionary income. Otherwise, if you're working for someone else, it will be commensurate with your new cost of living expenses, and you may find yourself in the same economic situation as the one you left.

CHOOSE YOUR WEAPON

TOOLS OF THE TRADE

There are so many exciting budgeting tools for individuals today, and this is one area where technology has undoubtedly proven itself useful. (For other examples of amazing technology, enter iTypewriter, Useless Box, or Foot Tanner in your preferred search engine).

Before you get any further in this chapter, I also want to tell you that there are no paid product placements anywhere in this book. I received zero dollars for any companies that may be mentioned herein, so everything I say is my opinion from my own experiences.

So as I sit here and type on my zippy Apple laptop eating this delicious Subway veggie sub, you can rest assured that nothing, not even the smoky and spicy glass of 2009 Firestone Pinot Noir in my hand, is mentioned because I was paid to. Okay, but seriously: no money. #eatfresh

In the old days, good household budgeters used file folders, with each file folder representing a particular expense. Receipts were saved and filed into the folders they represented at the end of each day. Usually, a hand-written cover sheet tabulated the expenses for a given month, and so you knew how much more you could spend in a given expense category.

This is a great manual system, yet in it exists a disconnect between spending and projections or financial goals.

Some people use the "balance the checkbook" method, which is a useful reconciliation process, but hardly a financial plan that assists with budgeting.

We all know the person who uses their daily bank balance to manage how much they can spend. Suddenly, a check comes through that they forgot about, and they're wiped out with some sweet bank fees to boot. Balancing the checkbook could help prevent this, if it's done often enough, but most people procrastinate and the process falls apart.

Excel is one of the universe's finest tools, and there are a huge number of people out there using spreadsheets and basic formulas to stay on track. I built an Excel workbook for budgeting in 2009, and shared it with my friends with great success. It requires just moderate Excel skills, and can be customized to the needs of almost anyone. I have since retired that Excel tool.

For the past couple of years, some brilliant apps have been emerging, and they are genuinely exciting. Personal finance software is nothing new, but the ability for these programs and apps to pull data from your bank, loan, investment and credit card accounts is relatively new and such a time saving benefit. Personal finance software is now becoming commonplace, and there are no more excuses for not being on top of your game.

You have options that are more encompassing, more efficient, more portable, and tremendously more insightful than other, more manual methods. Best of all, most of them are free! To name a few, there are Mint, Nerd Wallet, YNAB, Every Dollar, Pocket Guard, Personal Capital, and many more. New ones come out every month.

Most of these personal finance tools offer free smartphone apps as well. In my family's case, a big benefit of these apps is that they provide a shared means for me and my wife to efficiently manage our family's budget and finances from our phones. We each downloaded the free Mint app and log in with the same credentials.

When she marches into the mall, one glimpse at her phone tells her how much she cannot spend on shoes. When I stroll into the music store, my phone tells me how much I cannot spend on a Tommy Lee-sized drum rack for my electric kit.

Getting someone like my mom to trust these cloud-based solutions can be challenging. She is concerned about privacy, and would surely not like having her financial information stored in the cloud.

But these concerns are rooted in the often-irresponsible news reports of computer viruses and people giving their life savings away to overseas princes.

Technology and security, let alone credit card fraud protections, have made these apps safe and secure. In fact, these sites can only read your information, and neither you nor they can transfer money or perform any type of financial transaction.

It's a personal decision that you need to make on your own, but be sure you have the proper facts before making that decision. As for my mom, hopefully she reads this book and her trust shifts enough to try one of these amazing tools.

Mint.com is a powerful tool, and the primary one I've been using for the past two years. Intuit bought Mint in 2009 for $170 million, and the software has made additional advancements since then. I love everything about Mint and use it all the time.

I read a review where someone complained that Mint.com offered them financial tools and products as part of their service. This is how Mint generates revenue, which seems fair, since I'm using their product for free.

Most Mint users would probably even pay a small monthly fee for the software. But how this could be bothersome to someone is beyond me. The offers they have and advice they give, such as higher-earning savings accounts, is valuable for people to have put in front of them.

Mint and others show you how your spending categories compare to other similar users in their database. This is an extraordinarily useful tool in maintaining and keeping tabs on your spending.

One of my favorite aspects of these software solutions is that you do not need to manually reconcile your accounts. It was this tremendously tedious reconciliation procedure that made me ditch Quicken a few years back. Mint, for example, organizes your spending into categories. I simply review and make any changes that might be necessary, but usually they choose correctly.

With most of these app solutions, you see and monitor every transaction that flows through your accounts.

However, you don't need to sit with a bank statement and check off each item. For a business with a large number of transactions, this is of course a crucial process. For most individuals, and for me, it is not.

Each platform seems to have its strengths and

weaknesses, and there have likely been even more players enter the market between the time I'm writing this and the time you're reading it.

The focus of this book is not to say that one platform is better than another, and I have not tried them all. Explore, read reviews, and whatever you choose, try two and close down the one you like the least. If you're still unhappy, try another, and keep moving until you've found a platform that is fun and tells you everything you need to know to keep your plan on track

GET BUDGETIZED

DO WHAT?

The actual budget process involves a lot of trial and error, but guidelines can help get you started. I am going to discuss this section as if you are using one of the online software tools.

If you're using an Excel workbook or another manual system, only select pieces of the following will apply. You'll know what to pass over. But I highly recommend that you try using one of the online tools as well, as there are benefits for online budgeters that simply don't exist when using a spreadsheet.

Once you setup up your login, the first task is to load in all of your accounts: checking accounts, savings accounts, retirement accounts, credit cards, charge cards, mortgages, investment accounts, car loans, boat loans, valuable assets…everything.

Say, for example, you have a mortgage and you connect to that account so your mortgage balance is showing. This alone will paint a depressing picture of your net worth, while also an inaccurate one. Be sure to add, in this example, your home's value as an asset.

Your goal is to have both your mortgage account of $250,000 and your house as an asset with a market value $325,000 listed, thus reflecting a net positive value of $75,000. The same thing applies to any other assets you might own. If you have a car loan, connect that account, but don't forget to add your car as an asset at its fair market value. This doesn't apply if you lease your car, because you do not own an asset; you are simply leasing the car.

The next step involves determining your income, and this is the very first budget you create! Be careful with this step, and be as absolutely conservative as possible.

As you read a few sections ago, create your income budget so that you have no reasonable chance of ever coming in under-budget in terms of income.

Let's say you have a 9-5 job, and that job includes an annual bonus. Sometimes this bonus is big and sometimes this bonus is small. If it is not guaranteed, exclude it from your income budget.

Then, if you do get a bonus at the end of the year, you will have some extra money to invest, pay off debt, or use for that dream vacation to Tarragona, Spain for the human tower competition.

BUDGETING YOUR EXPENSES

You hear about a lot of rules and ratios for household budgets. There's one rule in particular that I want to bring attention to, and that is the 30 percent rule.

The 30 percent rule says that you should spend no more than 30 percent of your gross, pre-tax income on housing. So if your salary is $50,000 per year, then your base housing costs should not exceed $1,250 per month. ($50,000 times .3, and then divide that result by twelve to arrive at your monthly ceiling)

This is not always an easy rule to follow, and it is remarkably easy to sign up for a situation that reaches closer to 40 percent or even [eek!] 50 percent of our gross income. Going beyond the 30 percent zone creates a way of life where people are "slaves to their mortgages," and problems inevitably introduce themselves.

The great housing collapse that started to show its ugly face in early 2007 could have been avoided if the industry had simply followed the 30 percent rule.

People had future expectations of increased wealth and overly optimistic future valuations of their properties. It didn't help that loans were being churned out as if Henry Ford were in charge, and being given to people who clearly could not afford the mortgage they were committing themselves to. The 30 percent rule was grossly ignored by parties on both sides of the now-moldy picket fence.

If it helps, make a list of everything you need to buy or do in the next twelve months. I currently live in LA, but my entire family is in Chicago, where I am from. Trips to see them can be expensive, especially now that there are three of us, so including these expenses in my household budget is important.

Whether it's a new transmission for your car or last Christmas's charge card balance, write these items down and divide by twelve to calculate your monthly expense. Some online financial tools can also assist with this "setting goals" process. You'll read about them later.

FIXED EXPENSES

You will continue creating budgets for your fixed expenses, such as car payments, insurance, and rent or mortgage payments. These expenses are guaranteed bills that are going to be paid each month with little to no change in amount, unless you change something.

The reason you budget for your fixed expenses first is that fixed expenses are usually more "need" than "want," and variable expenses allow you the most control in modifying them. This isn't to say that you may not have stretched yourself too far on your current apartment, but let's consider that to be a fixed expense for this exercise.

After entering your income and fixed expenses, stand back and see where you're at. This view is an important analysis for you to do.

VARIABLE EXPENSES

Next in line are your variable expenses. Variable expenses have the ability to vary in amount such as entertainment, restaurants, groceries, household items, transportation, clothing, and kids.

As a father, I can attest that kids are expensive. And, like it or not, if you have kids, you are going to have variable expenses related to their goings-on. I am not referring to more fixed expenses, like clothing or food, but more so school projects, sporting expenses, banjo lessons, or a gift for a friend's birthday party.

Every penny you spend should have a place in your budget. This includes gifts for holidays and birthdays, pocket money, even parking tickets, if you have challenges moving your car in accordance with the tiny, poorly labeled signs that adorn most city streets. Capture it all.

You also may not think of pocket money as an expense, but you always spend money for things you weren't planning on buying, and everyone buys on impulse, some more than others. You may stop for a coffee or buy something for your significant other that you happen to come across.

You also want to allow yourself a reasonable buffer. If your monthly take-home income is $4,000, then budget your expenses totaling $3,800. You want to squish how much you spend as much as you can comfortably, and the rest will be there for saving and investing.

Another aspect of many of these budgeting tools is the ability to set up goals. This is how you choose to allocate any extra income in your budget. Perhaps it's saving for a child's college, buying a car, or building your savings; create a goal using the software, and you can track your progress easily. Of course, this also serves as an excellent buffer for months where, although rare, you dared to exceed your budget.

Some of these budgeting tools will allow you to set up each budget as a fixed or rolling budget. With a fixed budget, you allow yourself a certain amount to spend in a particular category. When the new month begins, the budget restarts at $0.

Rolling budgets will carry forward the net amount or deficit from the previous month. Grocery budgets are often a good use of a rolling budget, because you may not always buy your groceries for a given month entirely within that month.

Maybe you went on a grocery shopping spree to take advantage of a sale on Norwegian shrimp, and although you made the purchase in April, the food will be consumed in May. A rolling budget will account for these overlaps and keep you on track.

GETTING OUT OF DEBT

This book does not address specific "get out of debt" strategies, because that could be the focus of an entire book of its own, and our focus is on budgeting and growth. This book also bypasses a lot of the specific topics that most readers might already know.

If you're in credit card debt, of course the best strategy is to get out of it. However, since debt payments are part of a budget, I need to address this topic. The general advice I offer people in credit card debt is as follows:

- Start spending less than you earn
- Establish a small emergency cash fund
- Halt the creation of further debt
- Pay off any smaller balances first
- Look for reduced interest rates
- Self-educate and grow your income
- Budget, and never let it happen again

With that being laid out, this book will now enter this topic in terms of how to budget your debt payments. One of the niceties of budgeting for debt payments is that you are reducing the negative impact of compound interest.

With each payment, you can feel good not only that you're paying down your debt, but also that you're slowing the amount of interest you will need to pay back.

Additionally, your debt payments can be thought of as a transfer, rather than an expense. You are taking money from your cash account and relieving a liability. In reality, you're paying for a past expense, but still it feels damn good.

When you make those credit card payments, you have several reasons to cheer yourself on, and it's not just cash out the door, because you're saving future interest expense, too.

ONLY THE BEST

It's time for you to dive in. Get your budget set up and, once you're happy, come back to this book and start at the chapter immediately following this one.

What seems like an awful process is actually fun and encouraging, especially when you see your money allocated toward the things you value most.

If you're already set up and running with a budgeting system, now is your chance to modify your budget with some of the things you've learned in this book.

But before you close this book and move on to setting up or modifying your budget and financial plan, you need to consider something I call the "New Year's Effect."

You know how the gyms are packed with people in shiny workout gear during that first week of January, and then the wait for the elliptical machine becomes nonexistent by about mid-March? You don't want that to happen with your financial plan and budget.

Make sure your goals are realistic, and that you are committed to them. If you're a person who loves spending time out, do not kill your entire entertainment budget for the year. Unless you're committed to a serious lifestyle change, you will fail and set yourself up for guilt and avoidance of your improved financial mindset.

If you're a person who loves shopping, but carries credit card debt, you should make drastic changes, but not so drastic that you can never buy anything ever again. Allow yourself a conservative treat within your new budget so that you're motivated to stick with it.

Another process to be aware of is that your budget will be updated as you go. It is not a disappointment to realize after two months that you need to allocate more toward groceries and less toward movies each month. This is what everyone does, and it's what the biggest companies do, too. Budgets are rarely perfectly static, and the reason is simply that things change.

Having said that, my advice is to allow yourself changes that bring you closer to your long-term life and financial goals. I would not recommend, after a month, that you realize your love of the most expensive makeup products are the only ones that suit you, and that you need to take on more credit card debt to support your face's favorite flavors.

I would recommend that if you realize that having the extra expense of a premium sports package is something you genuinely look forward to after a hectic week at work, then increasing your TV budget and decreasing, perhaps, your travel budget, would make for a worthy update.

Your budget should represent your values, and if you keep

that in mind, this whole process will be a lot smoother, easier, and more fulfilling.

Okay, you are dismissed. The next chapter is waiting for you upon the successful setup or update of your plan. Enjoy, and I look forward to your return.

INCREASE INCOME, SAVE & INVEST

SHOW ME DA MONEY

This part of our financial plan is about maximizing income, saving, and investing. This step comes after we've made our cuts for a reason, and that reason is so that our increased income is not misused and so that it does not arrive before you have a stiff handle on your finances.

Now that you've explored your values, reduced your expenses, and implemented a budget tool to measure your performance, it's time to increase income, save, and invest. But first, one more step.

CLEAN HOUSE

This is not a metaphor. Vast riches may be lying unappreciated in your home, and what's better than organizing while also bringing in money?

Sell things you don't use at a garage sale or online. Donate old clothes. Recycle or donate old electronic devices, like cellphones and computers. A new budget and vision are great companions to an organized mind and household.

Now onto the metaphor: this is the time to say *auf wiedersehen* to anything unnecessarily tying up, wasting, or eating your money.

Maybe you have a business that's been burning your money and providing little or no return.

Maybe you have a friend from grade school who's been sleeping on your sofa for the past two months, who is putting you over budget by eating all of your food.

Maybe you have a significant other who doesn't share your vision of increasing wealth, and instead spends the available money on expenses instead of assets that can work for you while you sleep.

Maybe you have some investments that are best to sell off now, which can provide a tax advantage. This won't help in a pretax portfolio, like a 401k, but losses can be a positive activity in a post-tax account, especially if you have taxable income to offset it. There are strategies where you can, for example, sell your underperforming S&P 500 index fund, take the loss, and immediately buy an S&P 750 fund to ride the wave back up. The S&P 750 closely mirrors the 500.

This is going further into investing than this book was meant to go. The point is that whatever the situation, this is the time to reevaluate and make some tough decisions. You will thank yourself later and forever.

INCREASE INCOME

Who doesn't wish they earned more money? Most everyone does, but not everyone wants to put in the consistent effort to do so. Be healthy, build good habits, self-educate, grow, automate, and repeat! That is the formula.

Self-education is critical if you want to get ahead, and you're already doing an awesome job of that by reading this book. Read more, listen more, network more. Focus on growth and on becoming a person with better habits. This makes you more valuable in the marketplace.

Your real competition is yourself. If that statement doesn't ring true, you are either not giving yourself short- and long-term goals or you're not setting your goals high enough.

When it comes to income, even slight increases today can lead to major gains later. A $2,000-per-year raise at your job may not sound like a lot, but over time, if you put that money to work instead of wasting it on expenses, that $2,000 can become $30,000+ by the time you retire. Or $10,000 by the time you want to buy a house.

So, get that raise. Ask for that bonus you deserve. Make yourself more valuable, and network to increase your chances of encountering new opportunities and becoming a bigger asset to your employer and the marketplace. Increase your luck by improving yourself!

To really give your income a boost, you need to stop trading your time for money and instead find a way to make money while you sleep. This doesn't mean that you need to quit your job. You can still start a business or launch a side hustle on evenings and weekends, after you're done kicking a$$ at your day job.

Create a product and sell it online. Invest your money. Invest in yourself. Automate everything. All of these are excellent ways to earn money while you sleep. They don't teach this in school!

There are opportunities for you to earn more money if you simply muster the confidence, persistence, and energy to do so. And even moderate increases in your income can have an immense impact on your financial future. You will learn more about that at the end of this chapter.

SAVE & AUTOMATE

Saving money needs to be part of your budget plan. In other words, your budget needs to include room for savings. The only exception would be if you need to get out of debt first. But even then, I recommend you create a little savings buffer for emergencies. If you have debt, don't skip this section!

When you create your budget and have money left over...that's your savings to invest. The problem is that you may see the extra cash in your account and feel inclined to spend it.

What can you do to avoid this, you ask? Automate your savings!

Just like how you might schedule a bill payment, you should setup an automated transfer of money from your checking account into your savings account. Do this each payday, or weekly, or whatever works best with the timing of your situation. This way, your extra money is automatically moved to your savings account, where it can be put to work for you.

There is a lot of science behind the power of automation and how it helps develop our habits. If you leave it up to yourself to make that transfer to savings manually every two weeks, it is much less likely to happen, especially over an extended period of time.

If you receive a paycheck, schedule the transfers to savings to occur on the day your paycheck lands in your accounts. That way, you don't have the risk of the Wealth Effect kicking in when you see your checking account balance. Get those savings transfers automated right now.

THE WEALTH EFFECT

The Wealth Effect is an increase in one's spending based on perceived but unrealized gains. This is most often driven by the housing market. It basically means that when a market is doing well, people have more confidence and spend more.

Overall, this is not a good thing. For example, you may notice that your 401k is doing great and you feel wealthier because of it, even though you have no more money to spend than you did in the period prior. Still, the Wealth Effect takes over and tells you to buy a new TV or a diamond tea bag, because you *feel* wealthier. Suddenly you find yourself in debt, because although you felt like you had more money, you didn't really have more money.

What's important is that you be aware of the Wealth Effect, so you can identify it when it hits and stop it before it drives you towards a bad decision.

INVEST & AUTOMATE

Investing is the surest way to increase wealth. You may think of retirement when you think of investing, but investing can also be for the short term. Your short-term goal could be to save for a vacation or a down payment on a home or a vacation home.

You do not need a broker to invest wisely. In fact, brokers are not obligated to have your best interests in mind at all, and can lead you toward more expensive instruments that earn them a higher paycheck. Even an honest broker can sometimes put their interests first and not resist temptation. So don't do it.

If you insist on outsourcing your investment decisions, seek out a fiduciary. Fiduciaries are required by law to act in your best interest.

There are of course honest brokers out there. My

grandfather was a stockbroker, working for Edward Jones in St. Louis for forty-three years until he retired in 1987. He had an amazing reputation for his honesty and dedication to his customers.

I recall sitting in his living room with him when I was a kid. He would smoke his pipe, and on the TV would be the financial news. Stock tickers ran across the bottom of the screen. It was all so cool to me. He bought me my first portfolio when I was about twelve years old, and filled it with a few NewsCorp [NWS] shares. This was 1980-something, and I remember checking the stock price in the paper each Sunday. And holy @&%—typing that last sentence made me feel really old! At least my mom says I still look youthful. I have that going for me.

You don't need a grandpa who watches the stock tickers, or a small portfolio when you're young to be good at investing. I was a kid, and my grandpa and I did not discuss investment strategies or anything about money that I recall. But he did spark an interest that I would develop later in life. Much in the same way that I hope I am doing for you right now.

Most stockbrokers aside, unless you have a reason to outsource to a fiduciary, there are a few steps you can employ to get started completely on your own.

Many companies can open an investment portfolio for you. New ones pop up each day, and perhaps better ones will exist by the time you're reading this book. I currently recommend Fidelity to people, because they're nice.

Do a search for "where to invest in stocks" and you will find many options to choose from. Or contact a company like Fidelity, open an account, choose a low-expense S&P 500 Index fund, and automate your contributions to this account just as you now do for your savings account. Keep your investment money invested for the long-term, in sickness and in health. If history can be trusted, your money will grow. Get more conservative as you get closer to retirement. There are also index funds that are based on your retirement age. These are great if you want to "set it and forget it." Just make sure the expense ratio is low.

That's about as difficult as it needs to be. The key is to find investments that have low expense ratios and low fees, and to automate your contributions. What is an expense ratio, you ask? An expense ratio is an annual fee charged as a percentage of your investment. If you invest in a mutual fund with a 2 percent expense ratio, which is high these days, you will pay the fund twenty dollars per year for every $1,000 invested. A normal expense ratio on a mutual fund these days is usually around 1 percent, whereas index funds usually hover in the 0.2 percent range or lower.

Low expenses are what make index funds attractive. Index funds often perform the same as or better than mutual funds, the latter of which are managed by overpaid "experts" who have as good a chance at timing the market as a monkey.

That is not to say that an individual cannot do a superior job of valuing a company, such as has led to the success of investors like Warren Buffett. But index funds follow the same top performing stocks in the particular market of that index, and you get the benefits of that performance for much lower expense.

As you get closer to your goal or to retirement, you may reduce the risk in your portfolio via any number of methods, such as reducing the stock holdings you have. If you're reading this book, you're probably not near retirement age, so we won't dive further in that direction.

Through self-education, there are a number of other strategies you will discover, but the method above is the one I unofficially recommend to most people.

This is the point where I should make it clear that this is not investment advice, and you need to do your own research. I am not recommending certain stocks or funds, but giving you some ideas on where you can consider starting.

SOME STRATEGY

Time-value of money is the concept that says the earlier you receive money the more it is worth. This is due to interest you could earn or save and the higher cost of products later, due to inflation.

Maybe you're one of those people who receives a monster tax refund each year. Everyone loves a big refund check from Uncle Sam, but why loan the government your money? Adjust your withholding so that you come closer to breaking even. It's your money, and you deserve to have it work for you.

Although, as of this second edition, in 2020, interest rates are abysmal, compound interest is still your friend, and it's one of the safest tools for accruing wealth. But inflation will outpace your interest in periods of low interest. Keep your emergency fund in a savings account and put the rest of your money to work. A healthy emergency fund is three months of living expenses; and an even healthier emergency fund is six months of living expenses that you can easily access anytime.

Compound interest arises when interest is added to a principal amount, so that the interest that has been added also earns interest. This addition of interest to the principal is called compounding.

Be aware, though: compound interest can be an evil foe, too. Your credit card debt, for example, is compounded to the advantage of the credit card company, which is part of why it takes so long to pay down credit card debt.

Speaking of abysmal rates earlier, don't just accept whatever interest rate your bank throws at you. Get out there and hunt for the best offers. There are some first-rate, high-yield savings account opportunities if you do just a little research.

Remember that a penny doubled every day in your bank account is worth $5,368,709.12 in just thirty days. The science of compounding is an astronomically powerful tool.

REGULAR TUNE-UPS

CHECK YOUR PULSE

So you've gone a couple of months with your new budget, everything is moving along, and you're happy. This is when you want to really train your mind to look for cuts, whether you're rich or struggling.

This often comes naturally to people once they're utilizing a budget, because a little bit of savings on your car insurance, for example, means you can increase your budget somewhere else. *Win!*

Perhaps you can reach one of your financial goals more quickly or have a little more for dining out. Always be on the hunt for cost-cutting opportunities and adjust your budget accordingly. This thought process needs to become part of your routine.

Here are some common areas where you should look first:

- Interest rates on loans (car, home)
- Insurance (car, life, health, home/rent)
- Subscriptions (apps, TV, games)
- Diet (restaurants vs grocery)
- Bad habits (cut back on certain activities)

CONQUER YOUR CREDIT

One of the benefits of having and sticking to a financial plan is that your credit score will increase, because you're paying bills on time and not spending more than you earn or increasing debt.

The FICO scale ranges from 350-850, and the better your score, the better opportunities and interest rates you will have to choose from. But you know that.

On February 11 of 2013, the Federal Trade Commission said, "Five percent of U.S. consumers have an error on their credit report."

What you may not know is that once per year you can visit annualcreditreport.com and obtain your credit reports from the three major credit-reporting agencies absolutely free!

I highly recommend that you do this annually, to make sure all is accurate. If you find problems, get to work and tackle them without delay. If you need help, several services out there can help you for a small monthly fee. Be sure, though, not to fall for any services that offer to remove information that is accurate, as they are scams.

For example, if you bailed on your car payment for two months back in college, you will need to improve your credit around it and wait for those seven years to pass.

Another great strategy is to freeze your credit reports. By doing this, you will be issued a PIN number, and nothing can be added to your credit report without you providing that PIN. If you have kids, freeze their reports right now. They can unlock them when they turn eighteen.

This book isn't going to delve into credit much further, because you know you shouldn't use more than 25 percent of your available credit, and that you should pay off your balances each month.

You know that 15 percent of your credit score is in part determined by how long you've been borrowing. So closing credit accounts in good standing can injure your credit score. Of course, if a card charges a lot of money in annual fees, or annoys you in any way, then close it and move on. Just try to keep the age of your credit as old as you sensibly can.

The major concept I want to make a huge point of in this section is that available credit is not the same as the available balance in your checking account. Credit is not cash! It's obvious, and you know it, but so many people wouldn't carry credit card debt if they really understood this.

Many n00bs to the credit world get into trouble because they see a $10,000 card as $10,000 to spend. This is so untrue. Keeping your credit usage under 25 percent will help you maintain discipline here.

The credit and charge card companies want you to spend away, but don't let them draw you in. Interest charges on debt are part of how they earn billions per year. Pay off your cards each month, and never spend more than you can afford to pay off in that month. Overspending on credit cards can be especially tempting for young people, but don't do it! Avoid this to stay ahead forever.

CREDIT CARDS ARE NOT EVIL

I and a lot of financially savvy people use credit cards

every day. The difference is that financially savvy people will always pay off their credit cards in full every billing cycle. This can be a great way to increase your credit score, and also earn reward points for travel or cash back.

Reward points are not for everyone, and credit cards that offer rewards often come with hefty annual fees. You need to do the math to be sure that the rewards you receive exceed the expense of the annual fee. And if they don't, stick with cash.

I tend to pay every bill possible using a credit card, as long as there is no processing fee. I pay off the balance each month just as if I had used cash, except I usually earn a free airline ticket or two each year in rewards points. The cost of your rewards points is paid by the vendor who accepted your credit card transaction. So, somehow, the credit card companies always seem to win. And this is also why some vendors still do not accept credit cards. (Can't say I love that, though!)

You often hear about those people who denounce credit cards and use cash for everything, even big-name finance authors. That's great, if it works for them, but I enjoy the comfort of a credit card for the many reasons mentioned above. Just be responsible.

Decide what works best for you, and be extremely careful about the temptation to carry a balance. If you do not think you will be able to pay the balance of your card at the end of the month, or if the expense is outside your budget, do not take on the expense. Full stop.

INSURANCE

One area of expense that people sometimes eliminate is insurance. Although it is incredibly slim that you will ever need it, you always want to protect yourself with insurance. It seems like a luxury than can be deferred during tough times, but that can be a gigantic mistake.

A single mom recently told me a story about how she had just moved into a new apartment in a new city. To save money, she decided not to get renter's insurance for her apartment.

One month later, a boiling kettle was forgotten on the stove while she was running errands with her young child. She returned a half-hour later to a street full of fire trucks. What would have likely cost less than fifteen dollars per month turned into a $14,000 expense.

Don't skip checkups at your doctor. Don't skip dentist appointments. Don't skip liability insurance for your residence. Don't skip insurance.

These might all seem like expenses that can be deferred for a more comfortable time, but you are setting yourself up for a much bigger expense later if something goes wrong. As chapter one of this book states: lay it all out!

If you have kids, life insurance is critical. Get yourself a term policy, not a whole life policy. Term coverage is much less expensive, and you won't be making some broker and brokerage firm wealthy from your contributions. Even if you don't have kids, a small-term life insurance policy of $25k is a good idea to cover expenses in the unlikely event that you get sucked up in a tornado. Or abducted by aliens.

Serious note: there is such a thing as alien abduction insurance, and there are people who maintain such coverage. Don't be one of those people.

I fully realize insurance can be expensive, health insurance especially. And here in the USA, where so many of our costly health plans are tied to our jobs, it can be extremely tough to pay for health coverage when you don't have a job. While I do not have a solution to healthcare being tied to jobs today, there are options at the state level in some places, like here in California. Whatever you do, find a way to get some degree of coverage to make sure your castle is protected.

TIME TO GIVE BACK

Once you're able to, give back! If you do not have the cash to do so, give your time. Find a cause or three that you support, and donate however you can. Do your research, and be sure most of the money goes to the cause and not to administrative fees.

The planet and less fortunate kids are two areas where my family and I try to make improvements, but you could start anywhere. One of the businesses I am working on right now will eventually help school music programs so kids can get access to the arts via music.

Giving back through nonprofits will help make the world better while making you feel better. And it often results in a tax deduction, an additional benefit.

OUTRO

THE SECRET

As a musician, I know that sometimes the notes that are not played are the most impactful. This is because the melody provides our minds with the concept, and then every ear that hears the song will hear it just a little bit differently. That's the magic of music.

The goal of this book has been to present the philosophy behind the budgeting and growth process, and to make the read an enjoyable one. If you enjoyed this book, it may not be so much the words that I wrote, but the ones I didn't, and what came into your mind as you read.

This is why I chose this format over another technical step-by-step guide. The aim of this book is to be different and more effective. I hope I succeeded, and your reviews will make that determination. So please leave an honest review, wherever you bought the book! That is so important to me and all authors.

I would love to hear from you today. Visit me at **iamjimmiller.com**, where you can get more info, read my blog, see what I'm doing, and find links to my social networks. If you want to talk about anything in this book, hit me and other readers up in social media land. I enjoy hearing your questions and stories and read them all.

I also need to thank the editors at KAA for their thorough and technical review of this book. It's amazing how a creator can overlook mistakes, even though they built and reviewed their work tens of billions of times.

I hope you agree that budgeting doesn't have to suck. Create control, get more money, have fun, and achieve everything you want in life.

Bis dann!

Jim Miller

Made in the USA
Middletown, DE
07 December 2020